MARCUS M. RANDOLPH

the chronicles of...

"THE LOST POET"

Poetry-The Internal Window

No matter who you are, or where you are, life resides.
The facets of life surround us daily, and when faced with challenges, victories, or choices we internalize the results that are sometimes forever etched within our souls. The beauty is when we are able to look internally to find those untouched humanized experiences, put them into words, and tell the untold stories. Poetry is art. Words come from the depths of our being where no other can see, hear, or feel. The expressions of those in-depth feelings are brought to life for others to visualize with their imagination, and feel what another has internalized. Marcus Randolph, currently incarcerated in Tennessee, has done that in his book, *"the chronicles of...The Lost Poet"*. Visit his inner soul, and experience the art that comes alive from within during his challenging times.

Anita King, Editor and Design
Genesis Originals

Table of Contents

Poetry-The Internal Window
Acknowledgements
Introduction

Acknowledgements

First, I give honor to the Higher Being that controls my life, and my journey on this weary road. I want to thank my son for the love I see he has for me when I look into his eyes. Son, you are the reason I am standing stronger than ever. To my busy mother, who always has my back, and played a major role in in the process of this book. Mom, thanks for pushing me to be more than just a man by showing me how to be a great father. Mom, your love is always great. To my Queen, my wife, my heart, times have been hard, but somehow we find a way to make it through every time. My Queen, thanks for putting up with me all these years; love you. Last, but not least, I cannot forget those who take and have taken the time to read *"the chronicles of... The Lost Poet."* From the bottom of my heart, thank you. Thank you for helping make my dream come true. Also, I owe a special thanks to Anita King for her help in making the dream a reality.

Much Love,
Marcus M. Randolph
"The Lost Poet"

Introduction

Sometimes reality does not set in until you have lost the most important things in your life-family. As I sit in this dark world of a cage, I am able to reflect on life, both past, and present. I am able to see the errors of my ways, and the true love of family, and friends. Most importantly, being by one's self can bring you closer to God! Life is full of ups and downs, challenges and failures, but it is always up to you how to overcome these obstacles, and mold yourself into the person you should be. As a young black man, I have encountered many adversities. Some I conquered, but I let others take over my self-control. I lost faith. I did not lose faith in God. I lost faith in me. The bad decisions that I have made so far in my life have resulted in me being locked away like a dangerous animal. Away from my wife, my kids, my family, and my freedom. However, it is here in this dark, and dreary world where I am becoming the person I was always meant to be. I am becoming the person I need to be. I am being molded. In this book of poetry you will read about love, loss, and God. You will also read about the life choices, demons, and struggles that I, this individual, am faced with everyday of my life, and while being incarcerated.

"The ultimate measure of a man is not where he stands in moments of comfort and convenience, but where he stands at the time of challenge and controversy."

Dr. Martin Luther King, Jr.

ભ્ય
As Human As You!!

Yeah! I have felonies.

Yeah! I committed crimes.

Yeah! I broke the law,

And the end result, I did time.

I'm still just as human as you.

Yeah! My pants hang low,

Maybe lower than they should be,

That still don't give you power

To use your authority to harass me.

I'm still just as human as you.

Yeah! I have a past,

But, I'm not afraid to be myself.

So, I continue to live 'cause I been so close to death,

I'm still as human as you.

Yes! I did wrong,

But, I have weathered the worst.

I changed to be better,

So, stop grabbing your purse,

And idolize the fact that I'm not what I used to be.

I'm still as human as you,

But you're not even close to me.

Dedicated to Oscar Grant

We Are Not

Dedicated to Trayvon Martin

I am not a statistic--

I am not a figment of your imagination.

I am not just a number.

I am not a gang member.

You cannot disown me

Like, I'm not supposed to be here,

You cannot ignore me

Like my voice is hard to hear.

You cannot take what is rightfully mine,

But, I will show you the righteous kind.

Who are you to judge me

'Cause of the way I talk?

Disrespect, dishonor, and mistreat me

'Cause of the way I walk?

Label me a criminal, 'cause I wear a hoodie?

Shoot a young black male down,

And the verdict is not guilty?

This is supposed to be the land of the free,

And the home of the brave.

Instead, it is the land of the ignorance,

And, the land of the enslaved.

But, still I stand by any means necessary.

'Cause my people have survived

The death, stress, struggles, and worries.

So laugh at me if you like,

Point your fingers, make jokes,

And try to take my life.

I still stand as a man

Who is emancipated from the lies,

And your so called truth.

I'm proud of my people,

And, I am in love with what they do.

So, God bless my fallen brothers, and sisters.

This is for you, our heritage, and our race,

And for everyone that said we will be erased.

We are not statistics.

We are not just a number.

We are not a figment of your imagination

And, we are not all gang members.

But, we are the strength of which they speak

In the struggle of peace.

We are the voices of the world

And, we will forever be free.

ℰℛ

Our Last Stop

Our hearts have traveled thru the years,

Encountering all laughter, joy, and tears.

But, our love couldn't withstand the miles.

We try to force fate, and make it meant to be

But, our emotions had us so blind,

When the rain came we weren't able to see.

Traveling on this long road

With nothing left between us,

And when the journey finally ends,

It will be nothing but hate within us.

This is one trip we should avoid.

Why keep riding to the rhythm of love,

When our hearts tell lies.

Leaving honesty, and loyalty

In the dense fog before we arrive.

So, this is our final destination, our last stop.

This is the beginning of something

That will be beautiful,

Instead of something it is not.

This is our last stop.

OB

Soul Mate

How do I say, "I am sorry"

When I've never been sorry in my life?

How do I express my emotions

When my heart is cold as ice?

Never knew real love

'Cause I wouldn't allow it in my soul.

So, how do I say I'm sorry to love?

Because I don't want love to go.

How do I express my emotions with my soul?

'Cause I have emptiness inside of me.

How do I get love to forgive me?

'Cause my soul is where it wants to be.

❧

True Love

I was gone for a short time,

But, it seems like forever.

My heart was closed,

And my soul was cold 'cause we were not together.

Never know what the future holds.

But, I know God's got a plan

'Cause if it wasn't meant to be,

He would have never said, "Give me your hand."
To my wife, Love You

❧
Untitled

There is no more happiness.

Everything has evaporated in the wind.

I am tiptoeing thru this life of misery

'Cause I'm walking on eggshells,

Trying to make it to the end.

I can tell my focus needs more focus,

But my brain is blurry

From the sound of my heart's loneliness.

The echoes of my thoughts

Are overpowered by the drums of defeat.

Still trying to find the creation inside the

Destruction is no longer possible,

'Cause the destruction inside the creation

Is no longer weak.

❧
Killed by Love

Thump, Thump, Thump,

Is the last thing I hear right before by heart flatlines

From the defeat of love.

Submitting to the draining pain,

I couldn't stand anymore more,

"I surrender," is the last thing I said.

Then came my last breath.

What human would endure this kind of hell

Just for the sake of love?

Only a fool would believe something "magical"

Is everlasting.

'Cause only a sane human being knows

There's no happy ending.

You live, and you die.

Love lost, and love found,

But in the end, love is not forever!!!!!

ଔ

Confusion Within

Day in, and day out my situation is eating at my mind.

There is no way out.

Back in a place I done already seen--

How did I get myself in this problem?

Returning to a place I haven't seen

Since I was a teen.

Locked away like an animal,

But, still trying to remain human.

Trying to meditate on a better place

Not caring what people are assuming.

This confusion that I'm facing,

Between Me, Myself, and I

Is leaving confusion, and disillusion.

On which one should die?

Which one should stay?

And which one should go?

Which one got Me in this trouble?

While I tried to tell Myself, "No."

ल्ड

Misery

I got things I want to say,

And feelings I can't express.

Even though I am being caged like an animal

In my life, I have no regrets.

I have sympathy,

And I feel the remorse for those I hurt.

But, they'll never see my struggle,

Or understand my work.

They'll never hear the screams in my head,

Or the lost souls in my heart.

I got things I want to say,

And feelings I can't express.

When do my troubles end, and my life start?

I feel useless,

Just like the leaves falling off the tree in the fall.

Like a blind man trying to walk,

But finds nothing but a wall.

I am still at a standstill.

I got things I want to say,

And feelings I can't express.

But, it hurts so much I can't finish the rest.

I got things that'll never be said,

And feelings I'll never get to express.

❧
After the Aftermath

Listening to the sound of thunder

While I meditate to the explosive flashes of lightening.

Letting the drops of rain tease my eardrums

Like a kiss of love.

The whisper of the wind

Helps comfort the unsettling of my bleeding heart,

Blowing my invisible wounds away.

The crackling of the trees echo throughout my body

Like soothing music.

Helping me push back the pain

That seeps through my tears.

Then the sunshine, clearing up what I thought was peace,

Just to reveal the disaster that was my life.

ભ

Helpless

On one hand I've been blessed.

I have also been cursed.

I am a good man,

But, then again, I'm the worst.

Trying to live up to the name

That exceeds my expectation,

A name full of women

With myself as the exception.

Have I cursed my son?

To be born to this name,

To live, and walk in steps of shame?

How can I turn a boy into a man,

When I'm falling in line behind the boy

That wasn't a man?

I said, "I'm not like him!"

But we are identical.

All the mess he put me through,

It seems like my son will follow.

Years pass, and some things you should let go.

But the hatred won't let it leave.

My life keeps letting it live.

I'm sorry for putting this on you.

But you are my last hope.

My son, my only.

❧
Alone in the Dark

There is nothing left

Besides the unsound individuals I'm with.

The evil hasn't left, and the fear of fear is still lurking.

Time is at a standstill, and my life is on hold.

I hear the rain falling, and the sun never shines.

Who is this person who looks back at me

Through the reflection of the mirror?

I no longer recognize him.

He is only an image of what was a good man.

The pain in my heart is starting to consume me.

How do I get back to what was once life?

The unveiling of thoughts that I can't control

Is terrorizing my spirit.

I can't run, or hide.

I can't speak because I no longer have words.

There is no help, and there is no family.

There are no more seconds; there is only space.

Emptiness that contains all my fears.

I want to leave, but I can't.

Until I face these demons.

☙

Godly Love

How do I repay the greatest person God sent from above?

How do I repay the one that shows me everlasting love?

When my heart is broken, I hear your sweet voice.

I know sometimes you wonder about my decisions,

And my life choices.

Just remember no good deed goes unnoticed.

It might not seem like it,

But your words keep me focused.

Where would I be without you in my world?

I'll be lost, without a compass

Looking for a non-existent pearl.

You are the star that guides me

Through the storms on those

Unbearable nights.

I was blind, but with you, now I have sight.

"Thank you" does not explain the way I feel,

My life is yours, and because of you, I live.

You take away the pain, and carry all my sorrows,

You told me to live for today,

'Cause there is no tomorrow.

As I cry just thinking of your Godly soul,

With emotions so soft

And yet, so bold.

With wings of angels, and the glow of a dove,

How do I repay the person

God sent to show me how to love?

Thanks for everything.

I love you, and miss you so much.

Without you there wouldn't be me.
Love you, Mom

ଔ
Happy To Wake Up

I wake up with a smile

Just to keep from crying.

I wake up with hope

'Cause I have nothing else to hold on to.

I wake up with faith

'Cause only God can judge me.

I wake up with spiritual relief

'Cause soon my soul will be free.

I wake up with grace,

Because I am blessed to be alive.

I woke up, and prayed for a while

'Cause I'm thankful just to wake up with a smile.

❧
Who Am I?

I am the spirit put here to shine

When God said, "Let there be light."

Who Am I?

I am the father of two, a Prince, and a Princess,

And the husband of a Queen.

Who Am I?

I am the leader of many under me,

But a follower of none, not like me.

Who Am I?

I am more than a man

I am the image of God.

Who Am I?

I am the struggle,

I am the peace.

I am the one unchained from bondage.

Who Am I?

I am the meaning of Life!!!!

Who Are You?

❧
Left Behind

One year down, and a few more to go.

Concentrating on staying patient

While I'm traveling down this lonely road.

I started this with a family,

But somehow just ended up with myself.

Those that were supposed to be in my corner

Just disappeared like Houdini, and only I was left.

No goodbyes, and no sympathy letters were sent.

No last visit, no kiss on the glass;

No love was meant.

I became alienated, and exiled

By those who were supposed to be there.

Became a menace to society

By those who used to call my name

To protect them from menaces in our society

Now they don't know who I am.

One year down, and a few more to go.

Concentrating on staying patient,

'Cause I'm leaving them on this lonely road.

❧
These Are My Thoughts

I don't know where this path will lead me,

I don't know where I will go.

I see visions in my dreams that says loneliness,

And, when I open my eyes, I see fear.

It's hard being invisible while being seen.

Trying to teach one how to swim

While I am drowning.

Trying to find survival

'Cause I'm lost in the woods.

Who is to blame?

Who should I be mad at other than myself?

I found myself,

But it seems like I lost love in the process.

Fate should have been everlasting,

Instead of never seeing a beginning.

What I thought was true

Just ended up being my imagination.

Being blinded by what I thought was bright future,

Only left me powerless to the dark moment.

છ

Made in the USA
Columbia, SC
03 January 2024